# YOUR KNOWLEDGE HAS VALUE

# Trauma Narration in Patricia McCormick's Novel "Sold". The Impact of Human Trafficking

Lisa Thöne

**Bibliographic information published by the German National Library:**

The German National Library lists this publication in the National Bibliography; detailed bibliographic data are available on the Internet at http://dnb.dnb.de.

ISBN: 9783389029145
This book is also available as an ebook.

© GRIN Publishing GmbH
Trappentreustraße 1
80339 München

Print and binding: Books on Demand GmbH, Norderstedt, Germany
Printed on acid-free paper from responsible sources.

The present work has been carefully prepared. Nevertheless, authors and publishers do not incur liability for the correctness of information, notes, links and advice as well as any printing errors.

GRIN web shop: https://www.grin.com/document/1477005

University of Paderborn

Department of English and American Studies

Summer Term 2020

Seminar: American Trauma Narratives

# The Impact of Human Trafficking

# - Trauma Narration in Patricia McCormick's novel

# *Sold*

Lisa Thöne

Englischsprachige Literatur und Kultur
und Englische Sprachwissenschaft, 6th
semester

# Contents

# 1. Introduction

Told in a series of haunting vignettes, *Sold* is a harrowing account of sexual slavery. Alternating lyrical imagery with precise detail, McCormick gives voice to the terror and bewilderment of a young girl robbed of her childhood but who finds the strength to triumph (The National Book Awards qtdn. McCormick).

Trauma has many facets. It can have different scopes, which range from psychological to physical boundaries that were crossed. Nonetheless, how trauma is treated is highly dependent on the different individuals that face it. Thereby, trauma narratives fulfill a particular function: They tell stories about individuals getting traumatized and present their ways of coping with it, but at the same time, this sort of narratives reaches other individuals as well. These individuals will never have the same perception of the depicted trauma. However, trauma narratives help to feel emotionally connected and exhibit common structures of trauma, which help everyone to understand how trauma functions and to deal with traumatic situations.

Patricia McCormick sets out to the trauma resulting from human trafficking in her novel *Sold*, published in 2006. Here, readers learn about the protagonist Lakshmi's story of being sex-trafficked from Nepal to India. The author uses certain narrative techniques to crystallize what exactly the girl feels and thinks during her journey. Although she is an individual, readers are enabled to detect the stages Lakshmi goes through and get to understand the chaos in her mind.

Against this backdrop, *Sold* will be examined in terms of its narrative functions to capture the experiences of a traumatized individual, in this case arising through human trafficking. To get a general understanding of the main topic, the paper will start with a short excurse to human trafficking. After this, the stated purpose of the author and her novel will be outlined, to subsequently discuss how trauma narratives are set up according to Literary Studies professor Laurie Vickroy's theory, which approaches contemporary trauma narratives in her work *Voices of Survivors in Contemporary Fiction*. For the analysis part, this paper examines which functions of Laurie Vickroy's theory of trauma narratives Patricia McCormick fulfills in her novel *Sold*. During the course, the role of Lakshmi's language, which reveals the development of her thoughts and feelings, the impact of people accompanying her on her journey, as well as the aspect of creating reader empathy, will shape the discourse. Weighing everything up, the paper will arrive at a conclusion. In so doing, the overall purpose is to prove that *Sold* fulfills all of the three main functions of a trauma narrative by Laurie Vickroy because other characters either enhance or reduce the traumatic experience, Lakshmi's trauma is dependent on numerous aspects that interplay during the novel, and the reader is bound to the traumatic experience.

## 2. Background / Theory Chapter

*Sold* is a novel about human trafficking told from the perspective of a young girl, who has been brought from Nepal to India under false pretenses. Instead of working for a family, she is forced to work in a brothel. During the narration, the reader can sense how brainwashed and traumatised she is and how slowly she realises what is going on. Therefore, the process of becoming aware will be investigated. When some American men come to the brothel in order to rescue the girls they would hide instead of working along with them because they are told that these men would strip them naked and ridicule them on the streets. Clearly, this is a systematic strategy aiming to maintain the traumatic experience. Lakshmi would not be brought back to her family. Her family constitutes one element that keeps her striving and thus alive. The author Patricia McCormick claims that she did a lot of interviews with victims to get an inside into such structures of human trafficking so that she could then transfer the story to the readers ("Sold").

Generally, this paper is concerned with human trafficking from Nepal to India. In Nepal "[t]rafficking is illegal, but is still practiced" according to the organisation *womanstats* ("WomanStats Maps"). In India, it "is limitedly illegal and is practiced" ("WomanStats Maps"). Estimated 54 women and girls are trafficked across the border every day on average ("More than 50 Nepali Women and Girls …"). Often, family members sell children to "pay off a loan" but are paid less than agreed or nothing at all eventually (Dr. Thomas 44). "Lower casts and socially marginalised groups" are particularly affected by the issue of human trafficking (44). Through an earthquake in 2015 the situation became more drastic because many people lost their jobs and consequently take on untrustworthy offers ("More than 50 Nepali Women and Girls …"). Later on, many of them end up being trafficked ("More than 50 Nepali Women and Girls …"). Furthermore, female literacy in Nepal is 53.1% recently, which complicates spreading awareness ("More than 50 Nepali Women and Girls …"). Nevertheless, organisations with an agenda against human trafficking exist. They closely work with the Nepalese government and pass out potential victims at the border, but "the problem for Nepali women and girls is not restricted to cross-border trafficking" ("More than 50 Nepali Women and Girls …"). Another problem is that the border between Nepal and India is extremely long and India and Nepal share an open-border policy which makes it hard to control, but easy to traffick human beings (Dr. Thomas 44).

The topic of sexual trafficking becomes increasingly prominent according to Alison Jobe, a Ph.D. specialized on this topic (66). These stories can be told in various perspectives, may it be by "dramatists, journalists, or academics", which entails different responses (Jobe 69). *Sold* was written by a journalist, who openly attests that her novel is meant to increase activism against human trafficking ("Sold"). McCormick says that she wants to inspire other Americans to fight human trafficking all around the world ("Sold"). Her novel was inspired through an American photographer "posing as a customer so he could find young girls in brothels", which links these two worlds ("Sold"). Authors like her compose a whole entity in which they tell the story of trauma victims through their styles and techniques, which fulfill functions. Laurie Vickroy focusses on "social, situational, and narrative aspects" in her analysis of the functions of trauma narratives (*Voices of Survivors* 130). In addition to this, she consistently mentions in her essay how significant she considers the concept of the individual because every trauma story is unique (130). The author and character can display various attitudes and approaches decisive for the development of the story (130). Thereby, social relations play an important role (131). These contribute to a high extent to the psychological, traumatised status of characters, which is solved when the character is "offered clues and bits of memories to reassess survival" (131). In general, Vickroy defines trauma as a "dynamic process of feeling, remembering, assimilating, or recovering from [a certain traumatic] experience" (131). In this process, the individual, as well as its environment, determine the further course (132). Nonetheless, these two entities are interconnected and thus dependent (133). Dilemmas established upon imbalances of power can lead to anxiety for instance (132-3). Moreover, the genre of fiction enables an objective take on "the interweaving of the environment and human responses", whereby human responses can prevent the victim to strive further and get to cope with the situation (137). However, readers are capable to feel empathy and thus tend to engage the same emotions and reasonings like the individual, if the trauma text is "effective" at conveying the victim's thoughts and feelings (138). All this happens unconsciously (138). As the "social world" destines mental states, readers tend to recognise a pattern of thinking, which is denoted as "qualia" (139). Last but not least, authors of trauma narratives can portray the "collectively and situational - driven" traumatic situation in different ways, while the victim remembers it limitedly (140).


## 3. Analysis

The analysis builds on Vickroy's three general categories, namely the influences of other characters, the dynamic of the trauma process, and the creation of reader empathy. The latter two aspects are combined because empathy is triggered through the narrative strategy and technique that reveals the dynamic of the trauma process.


## 3.1 The influences of other character's on Lakshmi's trauma

Firstly, the influences of other characters are in focus due to their strong tie to Lakshmi's physical and mental health. For Lakshmi her mother Ama is a reason to strive for because the girl wants to afford her a tin roof and regains energy, when she thinks about being back with Ama. Surely, Ama is a role-model for Lakshmi. She encourages her to go to school and rebels against the patriarchic structures because she pulls out maize and a cigarette from the stepfather (McCormick 1, 27). At this moment, the girl and the woman are so uplifted and fortified that they fantasise about luxuries although their family lives in poverty (27-9). They long for freedom. Lakshmi "see[s], in that moment, the mischievous girl [Ama] was at [her] age" (27). Uncountable circumstances play together when it comes to the causes of trauma. In rural Nepal those overwhelmingly are caste and gender, where girls and women are neglected, even thou women are in the process of gaining economic power (Cameron 215). Since this, gender and caste are empathised in the Nepalese society to a questionable extent. Ama and Lakshmi thereby can be categorised as so - called "untouchable women [serving] as handmaidens" (215). McCormick thus fulfills one of the functions of trauma narratives elaborated by Vickroy: she thematises an imbalance of power, here between men and women, which is rooted so deeply that Lakshmi barely notices it, but is strongly struggling with it and questioning it (*Voices of Survivors* 132-3). This becomes perceptible when she asks Ama why women have to suffer but accepts it simultaneously by following all imposed duties like serving him tea and rubbing his feet at night (McCormick 8, 16). Also, this testifies the importance of structures. When such structures are removed, that can enhance trauma, no matter if they restricted the freedom of an individual or not.

Aspects like "women's lack of inheritance rights, preferential treatment of *males* over *females* in the areas of health and education, Hindu ideologies of the impure and dangerous female, and, in the extreme, female infanticide" become especially apparent in the novel *Sold* and combine in the figure of the stepfather (my italics, Miller qtdn. Cameron 216). Lakshmi is sent to the goat shed for a week because of her menstruation, which marks the gender - hierarchy between her and her stepfather, whom she is now forbidden to look into the eyes (McCormick 15). These circumstances entangle when she trusts him that she would be working for a rich family in the city but is sent to a brothel instead (52). She is considered impure because of her menstruation and her stepfather announces his entailed disrespect through joking with the other village-men (Cameron 218). Despite this, he makes her work at a place where she is forced to carry out *more impure* actions in the view of Hindu religion (220). In the later development, she learns that one girl, first forced to prostitution and then coming back home, is not welcome at home any longer (McCormick 193-4). This contradiction increases Lakshmi's trauma. Her basic trust in a close social relationship is not protected, but broken and taken advantage of to her disadvantage (Vickroy, *Voices of Survivors* 132-3).

Mumtaz dominates the girls with "[u]npredictability and *uncontrollability*", which are "predictive of more intense or prolonged psychological reactions to abuse" (Hossain et al. 2442). She is the figure through which it becomes ultimately evident that the increasing capitalist economy can be a particular hindrance for individuals of lower castes (Vickroy, *Reading Trauma Narratives* 181). In her former agricultural lifestyle Lakshmi experiences the advantages of slowly becoming enabled to work as a woman. New circumstances such as "male migration to India", "competition between mass-produced and local low-caste commodities", as well as challenged "social norms for female behavior" increase the freedom for women in Nepal (Cameron 225). However, Lakshmi herself is a young girl, who Ama therefore encourages to attend school instead of work (McCormick 1). In the brothel, Mumtaz takes capitalism to an extreme because she values capital over human beings and tortures the girls (Vickroy, *Reading Trauma Narratives* 181). Not only does Mumtaz *buy* human beings, but she wants to gain as much profit as possible through them (McCormick 92). Lakshmi gets locked away and is beaten every morning by the elderly woman, so that she would learn to obey (108-9). Moreover, Mumtaz tries to trick Lakshmi. She tells the teenager that she has to pay off 20.000 rupees, although Mumtaz noted down 10.000 rupees in her booklet and she confronts Lakshmi with the unfamiliarity of the city around them, so that Lakshmi will never dare to leave (105-6,132-3). This situation specifically demonstrates that Lakshmi and the other girls have to suffer from a complete loss of control over their lives. According to Vickroy, this entails "a deep sense of personal injury" (*Reading Trauma Narratives* 181).

Her new friend Shahanna *supports* of Lakshmi's physical and mental health. She hands her tea and water as well as condoms, which shall prevent Lakshmi from further physical suffering (McCormick 114, 123, 128). Additionally, Albrecht et al., who are sociologists, elaborated that verbal encouragement like hers can also affect a *physical* health condition (419). Shahanna reduces Lakshmi's uncertainty and uncontrollability of the situation, when she claims that "it [is] not so bad [there]" and supplies her with condoms so that Lakshmi can control getting genital diseases (McCormick 115, 128). What Shahanna does is "enhancing the individual's sense of efficacy or control, modifying judgements about the harmfulness of a perceived threat [like the *happiness house*], or identifying ways to escape from the threat", as Albrecht et al. write (427). Overall, individuals in a network of many, different people as in the *happiness house* can generally be said to have advantages contrasted to individuals in "overly dense, restricted and homogeneous ties" (440). Thus, the girls in the brothel, who differ in their age, attitude, and background, provide a variety of resources for Lakshmi. Lakshmi, for instance, gets many instructions for her well - being from the girls because every one of them has different knowledge and tips for her like how to receive sweets from men and how to prevent unpleasant smells (McCormick 141-3). The girls generally accept these offers for survival in the further course, which helps them healing faster (Vickroy, *Voices of Survivors* 131).

The 8-year old Harish stands for courage and hope. Lakshmi is ashamed when he catches her with his storybook, which derives from an "invalidated self - image" as Albrecht et al. termed it (428). Here, Harish reacts not only accepting but reassuring and affirming towards her because he grabs the storybook and immediately gives it back to Lakshmi when she drops it, instead of confronting her (McCormick 158). Adding to this, he later on offers her to teach her the words from the book (163). Like Shahanna, Harish becomes a friend, who helps the girl to rebuild a basic trust into the world. He accomplishes to decline and abolish various fears. With his general kindheartedness, he convinces Lakshmi of the *positive side* of the world. For instance, "he hands [her] a pencil. It is shiny yellow and it smells of lead and rubber. And possibility" (McCormick 182). This description and the metaphor highlight that he enables her to take the first steps away from Mumtaz and the brothel through teaching Lakshmi how to read and write in the language of the Americans who regularly come to the brothel to rescue girls. Since this, the pencil constitutes a symbol of hope. Furthermore, Harish tells Lakshmi about his American teacher and tries to clarify that Mumtaz lies about the Americans to detain the girls for the brothel (174). Lakshmi's unsound and doubtful thoughts, imposed by the manipulations of the traffickers and certain cultural influences, begin to transform into consciousness and awareness about her situation because of Harish's impact. "[C]ontradictions and inner conflicts" become dissolved and Lakshmi gains energy through her friendships so that she can finally find her way out of the traumatic situation (Vickroy, *Reading Trauma Narratives* 183).

## 3.2 How the narrative structure reveals the dynamic of the trauma process and creates reader empathy

Literary Studies expert Martina Kopf elaborated that the concepts *narrative, memory*, and *trauma* are "competitive and antagonistic" (41-2). Particularly *Sold* displays memory in a "highly emotional, contradictory, and fragmented" manner, which means that trauma can be detected by the absence of a complex narrative (Herman qtdn. Kopf 49).

Firstly, it stays out for discussion whether the author is either *implied* or a *teller* (Booth 429-30). These terms among other forms of authors are coined by literary critique Wayne C. Booth (429-30). On the one hand, Patricia McCormick invented the story and chose most details actively and consciously, which would make the author *implied*. On the other hand, she retells the story that many Nepali girls have to live through by intensely *thinking herself into* the role of the protagonist Lakshmi.

The discourse takes place in rural Nepal as well as in a big Indian city. In the beginning, Lakshmi summarises one year in the Nepalese mountains, whereby she declares that time there is "marked by women's work and women's woes" (McCormick 10-1). This unfolds how normalised it is for women and thus Lakshmi to suffer, which complicates her recovery from trauma. The repeated anaphor "[t]his is the season when" combines with children dying of different diseases, which pinpoints that Lakshmi is unable to speak about such events extensively (10-1). Occasionally, she explicates what the women do, like for example "silenc[ing] their own chuming stomachs", and describes the river as a "thundering beast" (10-1). The two metaphors' source is the *storm*, which mirrors the protagonist's confused inner state. At the end of this vignette, the girl reveals that the years in the mountains are a circuit that closes when the women prevent themselves from bearing babies by drinking "blue - black juice" (11). Since this, any hope for recovery is taken away. The brothel in the city enhances Lakshmi's trauma to a large extent, which is shown by ellipses. She recounts that "[e]ach morning and evening Mumtaz comes, beats [Lakshmi] with a leather strap, and locks the door behind her" (109). Lakshmi does not talk about what happens in between morning and evening because the events where she relates pain to are more crucial and ingrained in her memory. Vickroy calls this "limited remembering" (140). Despite her limited memory, the girl seems to remember the actions of passersby's in a more detailed way than her own because she can enumerate those (McCormick 109). The mere description of these passerbys is followed by her statement: "Not one looks up", meaning that she feels a lack of human nearness and human aid (109). Here, the reader is approached. The reader constitutes the *addressable other* (Kopf 51). According to Kopf, he is a witness, ideally an empathic one, so this passage can be read as an appeal to become active against sex trafficking and to generally pay attention to possible injustices in order to solve traumas like Lakshmi's (Kopf 43, Vickroy *Voices of Survivors* 138). In the further course of the novel, Lakshmi talks about the physical pain she suffers through the rape and therefore uses a remarkable number of nouns, which are: "the hurting", "the burning and the aching and the bleeding" (McCormick 125). In contrast to her physical status, she describes her surroundings by using positively connoted nouns like "[m]usic and laughter" (125). Clearly, the girl's overall fragmented language and her lack of adjectives and verbs testify that she does not want to withdraw the details of the rape, but wants to set the focus on the outcomes instead (Herman qtdn. Kopf 49; Vickroy, *Voices of Survivors* 140). While she is confronted with physical pain, other people around her are employed with celebrating and being happy. Furthermore, as she is *young* and *traumatised* at the same time, Lakshmi's language can be read as reflecting her inability to fully grasp what happens. According to Suzanne Keen, a Literary Studies professor, language should be the subject of analysis rather than being assumed to give total information (52).

Multiple situations reveal that Lakshmi has the character of an introvert. She is conflict – averse and unaware of injustices at the beginning of the story, whereas she begins to rebel against these in the latter course. When her stepfather wants to sell Lakshmi's cucumbers against her will, Lakshmi does not respond anything (McCormick 2). Moreover, as soon as the girl tells the reader about the subordination of women in Nepal, she barely uses judgmental words to do so (McCormick 10-1). Instead, it is left up to the reader how to engage the general situation of women in Nepal, which constitutes part of Lakshmi's identity. Not only does Lakshmi describe the situation without much emotion, but she "act[s] the part of a dutiful daughter" (8). The young girl gains a deeper sense of morality when she is trapped in the brothel and gets hurt there. At that point, she slowly becomes aware of her traumatic situation, which in turn enables her to start recovering (Vickroy, *Voices of Survivors* 139). Suzanne Keen talks about the "[s]tream of consciousness" in this regard (71). As trauma steers the victim's memory, the victim cannot be consciously aware of it nor control it (48). In this novel, the concept of the little vignettes highlights that. At some point in time Lakshmi's consciousness arises, which gets noticeable through "nonverbal or imagistic elements" (71-2). This is particularly demonstrable in the scene where the police stop by in the brothel to receive a bill from Mumtaz which should bribe the policemen not to rescue the girls (McCormick 159). Recounting it, Lakshmi claims that she does not understand (159). Through former dialogues the reader is directed to think that she does not understand the overall event, but indeed the teenager acknowledges that the policemen do not fulfill their purpose (159). To underline this rising awareness the phrase "I do not understand" stands in a single line and is then repeated in a larger stream of consciousness, which is: "I don't understand this city. It is full of so many bad people. Even the people who are supposed to be good" (159). Another linguistic element that signifies Lakshmi's confused mental state is the term *uncle husband*, used for the trafficker, who aims at hiding what he is doing (76-7). The traffickers, as well as her stepfather, try to undermine Lakshmi's awareness of her trauma when coining such terminology (Vickroy, *Voices of Survivors* 132-3). However, Lakshmi begins to solve problems in her own style. She learns the language of the city, does not start rivalries with the other girls, and is not offensive in her actions at all. Deriving from this, she believes in the *good*, which hinders her from becoming aware of her trauma at the beginning, but prevents her from becoming further traumatised equally.

Last, but not least, the *dialogic form* has to be taken into account. Keen makes clear that interaction takes place in a "polyphonic way, generating harmonies and tensions as well as out – and – out contradictions that may not be resolved in the text" (87). Like Vickroy, she argues that many different perspectives exist and appeals to scrutinize the different plot lines in a story because these paint at different points in time and different values of institutions among other aspects (87). Looking at *Sold*, the brothel builds an institution and is interconnected with the *human trafficking industry*. These stand in stark contrast to Lakshmi, Ama, and their lives in the Nepalese mountains. One scene in particular documents the contrast and Lakshmi's incapacity to understand it, whereas the traffickers understand, which aggravates the trauma of the young girl. Lakshmi's stepfather makes a deal with Bajai Sita, the woman working in the local store, and thereby claims that Lakshmi would "want(...) to go to work in the city" (52). During the process, Lakshmi mentions that she "feel[s] [her]self grow taller with his words", that her "cheeks flame with indignation", and that she "[would] do as [she] is told" (52). Nonetheless, she does not understand why the woman criticizes her lack of hips when she talks alone to the stepfather (53). This situation happens at the beginning of the story where the girl is filled with excitement rather than mistrust, which marks the dialogue between the three parties.

## 4. Conclusion

The thesis statement contains the idea that *Sold* fulfills all of the three main functions of a trauma narrative by Laurie Vickroy because other characters either enhance or reduce the traumatic experience, Lakshmi's trauma is dependent on numerous aspects that interplay during the novel, and the reader is bound to the traumatic experience. This is confirmed in the conclusion because all main functions are indeed fulfilled, but in a unique and individual way.

At first, it was explicated how prominent human trafficking is today, although many initiatives and changing laws are on the rise. Next, Patricia McCormick's purpose to authentically portray the trauma of many Nepali girls was shown, to then explain the functions of trauma narratives by Laurie Vickroy. During the analysis of the primary source with Laurie Vickroy's functions as a basis, broader structures of oppression like the social system in Nepal provided information about Lakshmi's situation, whereas more narrow structures like the brothel cause different mental injuries in the girl, but she finds strength through her new friends. All the people Lakshmi encounters on her journey do in some way influence her trauma. Ama is a *personal aim* that Lakshmi reaches for the whole time in the brothel, whereas her friends keep her alive, striving, and educated during the process. The stepfather is also a person Lakshmi wants to please but he devalues her, which affects her self – perception unconsciously and thus contributes to a high extent to the trauma. Rounding it up, it was shown how Mumtaz instigates Laksmi's ill mental state. In the second part, decisive stylistic elements for analysing a narrative were considered concerning Laurie Vickroy's functions of a trauma narrative. The analysis entails that Lakshmi is generally subdued and struggles throughout the whole story to get conscious and reassess her situation to start recovering. This gets transparent through her style of language and tends to create empathy and a will to become active within the reader.

Further research has to be conducted when it comes to the psychological impacts of victims of human trafficking and ways to heal these. Moreover, more analysis could focus on investigating individual character traits rather than forces from above because with the protagonist Lakshmi Patricia McCormick sets an example of how unique every single human being's identity is.

## Works Cited

Albrecht, Terrance L., et al. "Supportive Communication." *Handbook of Interpersonal Communication*. 2nd ed., edited by Mark L. Knapp and Gerald Miller, Sage Publications, 1994, pp. 419 – 49.

Booth, Wayne C. *The Rhetoric of Fiction*. 2nd ed., The University of Chicago Press, 1983.

Cameron, Mary M. "Transformations of Gender and Caste Divisions of Labor in Rural Nepal: Land, Hierarchy, and the Case of Untouchable Women." *Journal of Anthropological Research*, vol. 51, no. 3, 1995, pp. 215 – 46.

Dr. Thomas, Sarasu Esther. *Responses to Human Trafficking in Bangladesh, India, Nepal and Sri Lanka*. New Delhi, UNODC, 2011.

Hossain, Mazeda, et al. "The Relationship of Trauma to Mental Disorders Among Trafficked and Sexually Exploited Girls and Women." *American Journal of Public Health*, vol. 100, no. 12, 2010, pp. 2442 – 9.

Jobe, Alison. "Sexual Trafficking: A New Sexual Story?" *Gender and Interpersonal Violence: Language, Action and Representation*, edited by Karen Throsby and Flora Alexander, Palgrave Macmillan, 2008, pp. 66 – 82.

Keen, Suzanne. *Narrative Form*. 2nd ed., Palgrave Macmillan, 2015.

Kopf, Martina. "Trauma, Narrative, and the Art of Witnessing." *Slavery in Art and Literature: Approaches to Trauma, Memory and Visuality*, edited by Birgit Hähnel and Melanie Ulz, Frank and Timme, 2009, pp. 41 – 58.

McCormick, Patricia. *Sold*. Hyperion, 2006.

"More than 50 Nepali Women and Girls Trafficked into India Every Day." *FreedomUnited.org*, 11 March 2020, www.freedomunited.org/news/nepali-women-and-girls-trafficked-into-india/?gclid=CjwKCAjwtNf6BRAwEiwAkt6UQl1Kf0Q_9ZCTsdcV4j754d1W-whZ5uLuQkkbcSCYFPtvkUpBtN8GbxoCjjgQAvD_BwE. Accessed 26 August 2020.

"Sold." *Patriciamccormick*, www.patriciamccormick.com/sold.

Vickroy, Laurie. *Reading Trauma Narratives: The Contemporary Novel and the Psychology of Oppression*. University of Virginia Press, 2015.

Vickroy, Laurie. "Voices of Survivors in Contemporary Fiction." *Literary Trauma Theory Reconsidered*, edited by Michelle Balaev, Palgrave Macmillan, 2014, pp. 130-151.

*WomanStats Maps*, www.womanstats.org/maps.html.